Five ways

Personally

We are commanded to seek  22:19; Psalm 105:4, Is. 55:6; 17:17. But how are we to do this? His Holy Spirit is the one that leads us to Himself. His word, the Bible, and prayer are the primary means through which the Holy Spirit guides us to Him. That is why the Scripture is replete with the value of His word. Joshua 1:8; Psalm 19; 119:11; Isaiah 40:8; John 8:32 & 17:10; Romans 10:17; 2 Timothy 3:16,17, 1 Peter 2:2.

If you use and complete this guide you will have read the entire Bible in one year, plus one extra trip through the Psalms and Proverbs. This is meant to be used daily. First, ask God to show you something of the glory of Christ from His word. Our desire should be to move beyond the printed word into fellowship with the living Word, Jesus. Second, read the assigned portion of Scripture and then record your major impressions. Third, speak what the Holy Spirit shows you of His glory to someone else.

As part of a Men/Women in the word group

Finding Jesus is not just an individual exercise. It is an exercise done in community. The letter of First John is replete with statements and commands which make it clear that the result of finding Jesus is loving our brothers and sisters in Christ. This guide can be used in small groups of men or small groups of women. These groups should meet once a week for at least two purposes. The first is to hold each other accountable for seeking the Lord. As a result the primary question to be asked at each group meeting is, "How did the Lord speak to you through the reading of His word this week?" The assumption is that God is speaking and that the Holy Spirit speaks through His word. The goal is not necessarily to nail down a proper interpretation of a particular passage, although that may happen. The goal is to encourage one another in seeking the Lord in His word. The second goal is to establish relationships of love with each other as we share and pray for each other as we meet.

As a guide to family devotions

This guide could be used as a guide to family devotions. Depending on the attentiveness and needs of your family, you could read one or more tracks of Scripture. The first track read daily would take you through Genesis-2 Chronicles, which would be most of the Old Testament historical books. The second track would take you all the way through the New Testament. The third track would take you from Ezra through Malachi, which would be mostly prophetic material. The fourth track would take you through the Psalms and the Proverbs twice in one year.

As part of a Families in the word group

The Scripture is abundantly clear that the responsibility for the spiritual growth of the children lies with the fathers or the head of the household. Deuteronomy 6:4-9:

4"Hear, O Israel: The LORD our God, the LORD *is* one! 5"You shall love the LORD your God with all your heart, with all your soul, and with all your strength. 6"And these words which I command you today shall be in your heart. 7"You shall teach them diligently to your children, and shall talk of them when you sit in your house, when you walk by the way, when you lie down, and when you rise up. 8"You shall bind them as a sign on your hand, and they shall be as frontlets between your eyes. 9"You shall write them on the doorposts of your house and on your gates.

The Lord was not commanding the word to be physically attached to the hands, forehead, doorposts and gates as some ultra-orthodox Jewish sects practice today. Rather, He was commanding parents to be responsible to integrate His word into every area and task of life. The same principle is found in Ephesians 6:4: "And you, fathers, do not provoke your children to wrath, but bring them up in the training and admonition of the Lord. The training of our children to seek the Lord is meant to be a daily, moment-by-moment enterprise.

Far too often families are segregated to the point that in most churches in the USA today, parents expect the church to be the primary teacher of their children of the things of God. Yet clearly the Scripture lays this responsibility at the feet of fathers, mothers and grandparents. But how can we as a church come alongside heads of households to assist them in doing this? And how do we use the teaching gifts given to the body of Christ to aid parents to do this?

What if the church used this guide as a way of assisting fathers to teach their families to seek the Lord? During the week they could be reading the assigned portions to their families in the home. Once-a-week they could come together with other families to study word of God. The lesson would be designed by those in the small group who have a gift of teaching. They would prepare a lesson and lead the families in the group through the lesson which would be based upon the reading(s) done in the home during the week. If one followed this guide, they would read and studied the entire Bible in 3.5-4.0 years

As part of a "College in the Word" class

There are those who would like to learn more and take a more in-depth look at the word of God than what can be presented in family Bible study. What if the guide was used as guide to learning the Bible at a Bible College level? I would like to develop four different courses where one could use the reading schedule in the midst of the other type of functions to gain an equivalent to 12 hours of Bible College course work. The courses would include:

> Old Testament History Survey Genesis - 2 Chronicles
> Old Testament History and the Prophets
> Old Testament Poetry and Wisdom Literature
> New Testament Survey

How about you? Are you willing? What level of commitment are you willing to pursue?

January 1 Gen 1, Matt 1, Ezra 1, Ps 1

January 2 Gen 2, Matt 2, Ezra 2, Ps 2

January 3 Gen 3, Matt 3, Ezra 3, Ps 3

January 4 Gen 4, Matt 4, Ezra 4, Ps 4

January 5 Gen 5, Matt 5:1-26, Ezra 5, Ps 5

January 6 Gen 6, Matt 5:27-48, Ezra 6, Ps 6

January 7 Gen 7, Matt 6:1-21, Ezra 7, Ps 7

Favorite Verse this Week

January 8 Gen 8, Matt 6:22-34, Ezra 8, Ps 8

January 9 Gen 9-10, Matt 7, Ezra 9, Ps 9

January 10 Gen 11, Matt 8:1-17, Ezra 10, Ps 10

January 11 Gen 12, Matt 8:18-34, Neh 1, Ps 11

January 12 Gen 13, Matt 9:1-17, Neh 2, Ps 12

January 13 Gen 14, Matt 9:18-38, Neh 3, Ps 13

January 14 Gen 15, Matt 10:1-20, Neh 4, Ps 14

Favorite Verse this Week

January 15 Gen 16, Matt 10:21-42, Neh 5, Ps 15

January 16 Gen 17, Matt 11, Neh 6, Ps 16

January 17 Gen 18, Matt 12:1-21, Neh 7, Ps 17

January 18 Gen 19, Matt 12:22-50, Neh 8, Ps 18

January 19 Gen 20, Matt 13:1-3, Neh 9, Ps 19

January 20 Gen 21, Matt 13:31-58, Neh 10, Ps 20

January 21 Gen 22, Matt 14:1-21, Neh 11, Ps 21

Favorite Verse this Week

January 22 Gen 23, Matt 14:22-36, Neh 12, Ps 22

January 23 Gen 24, Matt 15:1-20, Neh 13, Ps 23

January 24 Gen 25, Matt 15:21-39, Esther 1, Ps 24

January 25 Gen 26, Matt 16, Esther 2, Ps 25

January 26 Gen 27, Matt 17, Esther 3, Ps 26

January 27 Gen 28, Matt 18:1-20, Esther 4, Ps 27

January 28 Gen 29, Matt 18:21-35, Esther 5, Ps 28

Favorite Verse this Week

January 29 Gen 30, Matt 19, Esther 6, Ps 29

January 30 Gen 31, Matt 20:1-16, Esther 7, Ps 30

January 31 Gen 32, Matt 20:17-34, Esther 8, Ps 31

February 1 Gen 33, Matt 21:1-22, Esther 9-10, Ps 32

February 2 Gen 34, Matt 21:23-46, Job 1, Ps 33

February 3 Gen 35-36, Matt 22:1-22, Job 2, Ps 34

February 4 Gen 37, Matt 22:23-46, Job 3, Ps 35

Favorite Verse this Week

February 5 Gen 38, Matt 23:1-22, Job 4, Ps 36

February 6 Gen 39, Matt 23:23-39, Job 5, Ps 37

February 7 Gen 40, Matt 24:1-28, Job 6, Ps 38

February 8 Gen 41, Matt 24:29-51, Job 7, Ps 39

February 9 Gen 42, Matt 25:1-30, Job 8, Ps 40

February 10 Gen 43, Matt 25:31-46, Job 9, Ps 41

February 11 Gen 44, Matt 26:1-25, Job 10, Ps 42

Favorite Verse this Week

February 12 Gen 45, Matt 26:26-46, Job 11, Ps 43

February 13 Gen 46, Mt 26:47-75, Job 12, Ps 44

February 14 Gen 47, Mt 27:1-26, Job 13, Ps 45

February 15 Gen 48, Mt 27:27-50, Job 14, Ps 46

February 16 Gen 49, Mt 27:51-66, Job 15, Ps 47

February 17 Gen 50, Mt 28, Job 16-17, Ps 48

February 18 Ex 1, Mark 1:1-20, Job 18, Ps 49

Favorite Verse this Week

February 19 Ex 2, Mk 1:21-45, Job 19, Ps 50

February 20 Ex 3, Mark 2, Job 20, Ps 51

February 21 Ex 4, Mk3:1-19, Job 21, Ps 52

February 22 Ex 5, Mk 3:20-35, Job 22, Ps 53

February 23 Ex 6, Mk 4l1-20, Job 23, Ps 54

February 24 Ex 7, Mk 4:21-41, Job 24, Ps 55

February 25 Ex 8, Mk 5:1-21, Job 25-26, Ps 56

Favorite Verse this Week

February 26 Ex 9, Mk 5:21-43, Job 27, Ps 57

February 27 Ex 10, Mk 6:1-29, Job 28, Ps 58

February 28 Ex 11:1-12:20, Mk 6:30-56, Job 29, Ps 59

Feb 29 Mark 7:1-23 (In non-leap years read this on Mar 1.)

March 1 Ex 12:21-50, Mk 7:24-37, Job 30, Ps 60

March 2 Ex 13, Mk 8:1-21, Job 31, Ps 61

March 3 Ex 14, Mk 8:21-38, Job 32, Ps 62

March 4 Ex 15, Mk 9:1-29, Job 33, Ps 63

Favorite Verse this Week

March 5   Ex 16, Mk 9:30-50, Job 34, Ps 64

March 6   Ex 17, Mk 10:1-31, Job 35, Ps 65

March 7   Ex 18, Mk 10:32-52, Job 36, Ps 66

March 8   Ex 19, Mk 11:1-18, Job 37, Ps 67

March 9   Ex 20, Mk 11:19-33, Job 38, Ps 68

March 10   Ex 21, Mk 12:1-27, Job 39, Ps 69

March 11   Ex 22, Mk 12:28-44, Job 40, Ps 70

Favorite Verse this Week

March 12   Ex 23, Mk 13:1-20, Job 41, Ps 71

March 13   Ex 24, Mk 13:21-37, Job 42, Ps 72

March 14   Ex 25, Mk 14:1-26, Job 43, Ps 73

March 15   Ex 26, Mk 14:27-52, Ecc 1, Ps 74

March 16 Ex 27, Mk 14:53-72, Ecc 2, Ps 75

March 17 Ex 28, Mk 15:1-25, Ecc 3, Ps 76

March 18 Ex 29, Mk 15:26-47, Ecc 4, Ps 77

Favorite Verse this Week

March 19   Ex 30, Mk 16, Ecc 5, Ps 78

March 20   Ex 31, Lk 1:1-25, Ecc 6, Ps 79

March 21   Ex 32, Lk 1:26-38, Ecc 7, Ps 80

March 22   Ex 33, Lk 1:39-56, Ecc 8, Ps 81

March 23   Ex 34, Lk 1:57-80, Ecc 9, Ps 82

March 24   Ex 35, Lk 2:1-24, Ecc 10, Ps 83

March 25   Ex 36, Lk 2:25-52, Ecc 11, Ps 84

Favorite Verse this Week

March 26   Ex 37, Lk 3, Ecc 12, Ps 85

March 27   Ex 38, Lk 4:1-30, Song 1, Ps 86

March 28   Ex 39, Lk 4:31-44, Song 2, Ps 87

March 29   Ex 40, Lk 5:1-16, Song 3, Ps 88

March 30   Lev 1, Lk 5:17-39, Song 4, Ps 89

March 31   Lev 2-3, Lk 6:1-26, Song 5, Ps 90

April 1   Lev 4, Lk 6:27-49, Song 6, Ps 91

Favorite Verse this Week

April 2   Lev 5, Lk7:l-30, Song 7, Ps 92

April 3   Lev 6, Lk 7:3 1-50, Song 8, Ps 93

April 4   Lev 7, Lk 811-25, Isa 1, Ps 94,

April 5   Lev 8, Lk 8:26-56, Isa 2, Ps 95

April 6   Lev 9, Lk 9:1-17, Isa 3, Ps 96

April 7   Lev 10, Lk 9:18-36, Isa 4, Ps 97

April 8   Lev 11-12, Lk 9:37-62, Isa 5, Ps 98

Favorite Verse this Week

April 9   Lev 13, Lk 10:11-24, Isa 6, Ps 99

April 10   Lev 14, Lk 10:25-42, Isa 7, Ps 100

April 11   Lev 15, Lk 11:1-28, Isa 8:1-9:7, Ps 101

April 12   Lev 16, Lk 11:29-54, Isa 9:8-10:4, Ps 102

April 13   Lev 17, Lk 12:1-31, Isa 10:5-34, Ps 103

April 14   Lev 18, Lk 12:32-59, Isa 11-12, Ps 104

April 15   Lev 19, Lk 13:1-21, Isa 13, Ps 105

Favorite Verse this Week

April 16   Lev 20, Lk 13:22-35, Isa 14, Ps 106

April 17   Lev 21, Lk 14:1-24, Isa 15, Ps 107

April 18   Lev 22, Lk 14:25-35, Isa 16, Ps 108

April 19   Lev 23, Lk 15:1-10, Isa 17-18, Ps 109

April 20   Lev 24, Lk 15:11-32, Isa 19-20, Ps 110

April 21   Lev 25, Lk 16, Isa 21, Ps 111

April 22   Lev 26, Lk 17:l-19, Isa 22 Ps 112

Favorite Verse this Week

April 23 Lev 27, Lk 7:20-37, Isa 23, Ps 113

April 24 Nu 1, Lk 18:1-17, Isa 24, Ps 114

April 25 Nu 2, Lk 18:18-43, Isa 25,,Ps 115

April 26 Nu 3, Lk 19:11-27, Isa 26, Ps 116-117

April 27   Nu 4, Lk 19:28-48, Isa 27, Ps 118

April 28   Nu 5, Lk 20:I-26, Isa 28, Ps 119:1-56

April 29   Nu 6, Lk 20:27-47, Isa 29, Ps 119:57-112

Favorite Verse this Week

April 30   Nu 7, Lk 21:1-19, Isa 30, Ps 119:113-176

May 1   Nu 8, Lk 2l:20-38,Isa 31, Ps 120

May 2   Nu 9, Lk 22:l-23, Isa 32, Ps 121

May 3   Nu 10, Lk 22:24-46, Isa 33, Ps 122

May 4   Num.11, Lk 22:47-71, Isa 34, Ps 123

May 5   Nu 12-13, Lk 23:i-25, Isa 35, Ps 124

May 6   Nu 14, Lk 23:26-56, Isa 36, Ps 125

Favorite Verse this Week

May 7   Nu 15, Lk 24:i-35, Isa 37, Ps 126

May 8   Nu 16, Lk 24:36-53, Isa 38, Ps 127

May 9   Nu 17-18, Jn 1:1-28, Isa 39, Ps 128

May 10   Nu 19, Jn 1:29-51, Isa 40, Ps 129

May 11 Nu 20, Jn 2, Isa 41,Ps 130

May 12 Nu 21, Jn 3:1-21, Isa 42, Ps 131

May 13 Nu 22, Jn 3:22-38, Isa 43, Ps 132

Favorite Verse this Week

May 14   Nu 23, Jn 4:1-30, Isa 44, Ps 133

May 15   Nu 24, Jn 4:31-54, Isa 45, Ps 134

May 16   Nu 25, Jn 5:1-23, Isa 46, Ps 135

May 17   Nu 26, Jn 5:25-47, Isa 47, Ps 136

May 18   Nu 27, Jn 6:1-21, Isa 48, Ps 137

May 19   Nu 28, Jn 6:22-44, Isa 49, Ps 138

May 20   Nu 29, Jn 6:45-71, Isa 50, Ps 139

Favorite Verse this Week

May 21   Nu 30, Jn 7:1-24, Isa 51, Ps 140

May 22   Nu 31, Jn 7:25-52, Isa 52, Ps 14

May 23   Nu 32, Jn 8:1-30, Isa 53, Ps 142

May 24   Nu 33, Jn 8:31-59, Isa 54, Ps 143

May 25   Nu 34, Jn 9:I-23, Isa 55, Ps 144

May 26   Nu 35, Jn 9:24-41, Isa 56, Ps 145

May 27   Nu 36, Jn 10:1-21, Isa 57, Ps 146

Favorite Verse this Week

May 28   Deut 1, Jn 10:22-42, Isa 58, Ps 147

May 29   Deut 2, Jn 11:1-27, Isa 59, Ps 148

May 30   Deut 3, Jn 11:28-57, Isa 60, Ps 149

May 31   Deut 4, Jn 12:1-26, Isa 61,Ps 150

June 1 Deut 5, Jn 12:27-50, Isa 62, Prov 1

June 2 Deut 6, Jn 13:1-20, Isa 63, Prov 2

June 3 Deut 7, Jn 13:21-38, Isa 64, Prov 3

Favorite Verse this Week

June 4   Deut 8, John 14, Isa 65, Prov 4

June 5   Deut 9, John 15, Isa 66, Prov 5

June 6   Deut 10, John 16, Jer 1, Prov 6

June 7   Deut 11, John 17, Jer 2, Prov 7

June 8   Deut 12, John 18:1-18, Jer 3,Prov 8

June 9   Deut 13-14, John 18:19-40, Jer 4, Prov 9

June 10   Deut 15, John 19:1-22, Jer 5,Prov 10

Favorite Verse this Week

June 11   Deut 16, John 19:23-42, Jer 6, Prov 11

June 12   Deut 17, John 20, Jer 7, Prov 12

June 13   Deut 18, John 21, Jer 8, Prov 13

June 14   Deut 19, Acts 1, Jer 9, Prov 14

June 15   Deut 20, Acts 2:1-21, Jer 10, Prov 15

June 16   Deut 21, Acts 2:22-47, Jer 11,Prov 16

June 17   Deut 22 Acts 3, Jer 12, Prov 17

Favorite Verse this Week

June 18   Deut 23, Acts 4:1-22, Jer 13, Prov 18

June 19   Deut 24, Acts 4:23-37, Jer 14, Prov 19

June 20   Deut 25, Acts 5:1-16, Jer 15, Prov 20

June 21   Deut 26, Acts 5:17-42, Jer 16, Prov 21

June 22   Dt 27:1-28:19, Acts 6, Jer 17, Prov 22

June 23   Dt 28:20-68, Acts 7:1-21, Jer 18, Prov 23

June 24   Deut 29, Acts 7:22-43, Jer 19, Prov 24

Favorite Verse this Week

June 25   Deut 30, Acts 7:44-60, Jer 20, Prov 25

June 26   Deut 31, Acts 8:1-25, Jer 21, Prov 26

June 27   Deut 32, Acts 8:26-40, Jer 22, Prov 27

June 28   Deut 33-34, Acts 9:1-22, Jer 23, Prov 28

June 29   Josh 1, Acts 9:23-43, Jer 24, Prov 29

June 30   Josh 2, Acts 10:1-23, Jer 25, Prov 30

July 1   Josh 3, Acts 10:24-48, Jer 26, Prov 31

Favorite Verse this Week

July 2   Josh 4, Acts 11, Jer 27, Ps 1

July 3   Josh 5, Acts 12, Jer 28, Ps 2

July 4   Josh 6, Acts 13:1-35, Jer 29, Ps 3

July 5   Josh 7, Acts 13:36-52, Jer 30, Ps 4

July 6   Josh 8,Acts 14, Jer 31, Ps 5

July 7   Josh 9, Acts 15:1-21, Jer 32, Ps 6

July 8   Josh 10, Acts 15:22-41, Jer 33, Ps 7

Favorite Verse this Week

July 9   Joshua 11, Acts 16:1-21, Jer 34, Ps 8

July 10   Joshua 12-13, Acts 16:22-40, Jer 35, Ps 9

July 11   Joshua 14-15, Acts 17:1-17, Jer 36, Ps 10

July 12   Joshua 16-17, Acts 17:16-34, Jer 37, Ps 11

July 13 Joshua 18-19 Acts 18, Jer 38, Ps 12

July 14 Joshua 20-21, Acts 19:1-20, Jer 39, Ps 13

July 15 Joshua 22, Acts 19:21-41, Jer 40, Ps 14

Favorite Verse this Week

July 16 Joshua 23, Acts 20:1-16, Jer 41, Ps 15

July 14 Joshua 24, Acts 20:17-38, Jer 42, Ps 16

July 18 Judges 1, Acts 21:1 -17, Jer 43, Ps 17

July 19 Judges 2, Acts 21:18-40, Jer 44, Ps 18, July 20

July 20 Judges 3, Acts 22, Jer 45, Ps 19

July 21 Judges 4, Acts 23:1-15, Jer 46, Ps 20

July 22 Judges 5, Acts 23:16-35, Jer 47, Ps 21

Favorite Verse this Week

July 23 Judges 6, Acts 24, Jer 48, Ps 22

July 24 Judges 7, Acts 25, Jer 49, Ps 23

July 25 Judges 8, Acts 26, Jer 50, Ps 24

July 25 Judges 9, Acts 27:1-26, Jer 51, Ps 25

July 27 Judges 10, Acts 27:27-44, Jer 52, Ps 26

July 28 Judges 11, Acts 28, Lam 1, Ps 27

July 29 Judges 12, Romans 1, Lam 2, Ps 28

Favorite Verse this Week

July 30 Judges 13, Rom 2, Lam 3, Ps 29

July 31 Judges 14, Rom 3, Lam 4, Ps 30

August 1 Judges 15, Rom 4, Lam 5, Ps 31

August 2 Judges 16, Rom 5, Ezekiel 1, Ps 32

August 3 Judges 17, Rom 6, Ezekiel 2, Ps 33

August 4 Judges 18 Rom 7, Ezekiel 3, Ps 34

August 5 Judges 19, Rom 8:1-21, Ezekiel 4, Ps 35

Favorite Verse this Week

August 6 Judges 20, Ro 8:22-39, Ezekiel 5, Ps 36

August 7 Judges 21, Ro 9:1-15, Ezekiel 6, Ps 37

August 8 Ruth 1, Ro 9:16-33, Ezekiel 7, Ps 38

August 9 Ruth 2, Ro 10, Ezekiel 8, Ps 39

August 10 Ruth 3-4,Ro 11:1-18, Ezekiel 9, Ps 40

August 11 1 Sam 1, Ro 11:19-36, Ezekiel 10, Ps 41

August 12 1 Sam 2, Ro 12, Ezekiel 11, Ps 4

Favorite Verse this Week

August 13 1 Sam 3, Ro 13, Ezekiel 12, Ps 43

August 14 1 Sam 4, Ro 14, Ezekiel 13, Ps 44

August 15 1 Sam 5-6, Ro 15:1-13, Ezekiel 14, Ps 45

August 16 1 Sam 7-8, Ro 15:14-33, Ezekiel 15, Ps 46

August 17 1 Sam 9, Ro 16, Ezekiel 16, Ps 47

August 18 1 Sam 10, 1 Cor 1, Ezekiel 17, Ps 48

August 19 1 Sam 11, 1 Cor 2, Ezekiel 18, Ps 49

Favorite Verse this Week

August 20 1 Sam 12, 1 Cor 3, Ezekiel 19, Ps 50

August 21 1 Sam 13, 1 Cor 4, Ezekiel 20, Ps 51

August 22 1 Sam 14, 1 Cor 5, Ezekiel 21, Ps 52

August 23 1 Sam 15, 1 Cor 6, Ezekiel 22, Ps 53

August 24 1 Sam 16, 1 Cor 7:1-16, Ezekiel 23, Ps 54

August 25 1 Sam 17, 1 Cor 7:17-40, Ezekiel 24, Ps 55

August 26 1 Sam 18, 1 Cor 8, Ezekiel 25, Ps 56

Favorite Verse this Week

August 27 1 Sam 19, 1 Cor 9, Ezekiel 26, Ps 57

August 28 1 Sam 20, 1 Cor 10:1-18, Ezekiel 27,Ps 58

August 29 1 Sam 21-22, 1 Cor 10:19-33, Ezekiel 28, Ps 59

August 30 1 Sam 23, 1 Cor 11:1-16, Ezekiel 29, Ps 60

August 31 1 Sam 24, 1 Cor 11:17-34, Ezekiel 30, Ps 61

September 1 1 Sam 25, 1 Cor 12, Ezekiel 31, Ps 62

September 2 1 Sam 26, 1 Cor 13, Ezekiel 32, Ps 63

Favorite Verse this Week

September 3 1 Sam 27, 1 Cor 14:1-19, Ezekiel 33, Ps 64

September 4 1 Sam 28, 1 Cor 14:20-40, Ezekiel 34, Ps 65

September 5 1 Sam 29-30, 1 Cor 15:1-28, Ezel 35, Ps 66

September 6 1 Sam 31, 1 Cor 15:29-58, Ezekiel 36, Ps 67

September 7 2 Sam 1, 1 Cor 16, Ezekiel 37, Ps 68

September 8 2 Sam 2, 2 Cor 1, Ezekiel 38, Ps 69

September 9 2 Sam 3, 2 Cor 2, Ezekiel 39, Ps 70

Favorite Verse this Week

September 10   2 Sam 4-5, 2 Cor 3, Ezekiel 40, Ps 71

September 11   2 Sam 6, 1 Cor 4, Ezekiel 41, Ps 72

September 12   2 Sam 7, 2 Cor 5, Ezekiel 42, Ps 73

September 13 2 Sam 8-9, 2 Cor 6, Ezekiel 43, Ps 74

September 14 2 Sam 10, 2 Cor 7, Ezekiel 44, Ps. 75

September 15 2 Sam 11, 2 Cor 8, Ezekiel 45, Ps 76

September 16 2Sam 12, 2 Cor 9, Ezekiel 46, Ps 77

Favorite Verse this Week

September 17 2 Sam 13, 2 Cor 10, Ezekiel 47, Ps 78

September 18 2 Sam 14, 2 Cor 11:1 -15, Ezekiel 48, Ps 79

September 19 2 Sam 15, 2 Cor 11:16-33, Daniel 1, Ps 80

September 20 2 Sam 16, 2 Cor 12, Daniel 2, Ps 81

September 21 2 Sam 17, 2 Cor 13, Daniel 3, Ps 82

September 22 2 Sam 18, Galatians 1, Daniel 4, Ps 83

September 23 2 Sam 19, Galatians 2, Daniel 5, Ps 84

Favorite Verse this Week

September 24 2 Sam 20, Galatians 3, Daniel 6, Ps 85

September 25 2 Sam 21, Galatians 4, Daniel 7, Ps 86

September 26 2 Sam 22, Galatians 5, Daniel 8, Ps 87

September 27 2 Sam 23, Galatians 6, Daniel 9, Ps 88

September 28 2 Sam 24,Ephesians 1, Daniel 10, Ps 89

September 29 1 Kings 1, Ephesians 2, Daniel 11, Ps 90

September 30 1 Kings 2, Ephesians 3, Daniel 12, Ps 91

Favorite Verse this Week

October 1 1 Kings 3, Ephesians 4, Hosea 1, Ps 92

October 2 1 Kings 4-5, Ephesians 5:1-14, Hosea 2, Ps 93

October 3 1 Kings 6, Ephesians 5:15-33, Hosea 3, Ps 94

October 4 1 Kings 7, Ephesians 6, Hosea 4, Ps 95

October 5 1 Kings 8, Philippians 1, Hosea 5, Ps 96

October 6 1 Kings 9, Philippians 2, Hosea 6, Ps 97

October 7 1 Kings 10, Philippians 3, Hosea 7, Ps 98

Favorite Verse this Week

October 8 1 Kings 11, Philippians 4, Hosea 8, Ps 99

October 9 1 Kings 12, Colossians 1, Hosea 9, Ps 100

October 10 1 Kings 13, Colossians 2, Hosea 10, Ps 101

October 11 1 Kings 14, Colossians 3, Hosea 11, Ps 102

October 12 1 Kings 15, Colossians 4, Hosea 12, Ps 103

October 13 1 Kings 16, 1 Thess 1, Hosea 13, Ps 104

October 14 1 Kings 17, 1 Thess 2, Hosea 14, Ps 105

Favorite Verse this Week

October 15 1 Kings 18, 1 Thess 3, Joel 1, Ps 106

October 16 1 Kings 19, 1 Thess 4, Joel 2, Ps 107

October 17 1 Kings 20, 1 Thess 5, Joel 3, Ps 108

October 18 1 Kings 21, 2 Thess 1, Amos 1, Ps 109

October 19 1 Kings 22, 2 Thess 2, Amos 2, Ps 110

October 20 2 Kings 1, 2 Thess 3, Amos 3, Ps 111

October 21 2 Kings 2, 1 Timothy 1, Amos 4, Ps 112

Favorite Verse this Week

October 22 2 Kings 3, 1 Timothy 2, Amos 5, Ps 113

October 23 2 Kings 4, 1 Timothy 3, Amos 6, Ps 114

October 24 2 Kings 5, 1 Timothy 4, Amos 7, Ps 115

October 25 2 Kings 6, 1 Timothy 5, Amos 8, Ps 116-117

October 26 2 Kings 7, 1 Timothy 6, Amos 9, Ps 118

October 27 2 Kings 8, 2 Timothy 1, Obadiah, Ps 119:1-40

October 28 2 Kings 9, 2 Timothy 2, Jonah 1, Ps 119:41-88

Favorite Verse this Week

October 29 2 Kings 10-11, 2 Timothy 3, Jonah 2, Ps 119:89-128

October 30 2 Kings 12, 2 Timothy 4, Jonah 3, Ps 119:129-176

October 31 2 Kings 13, Titus 1, Jonah 4, Ps 120

November 1 2 Kings 14, Titus 2, Micah 1, Ps 121

November 2 2 Kings 15, Titus 3, Micah 2, Ps 122

November 3 2 Kings 16, Philemon, Micah 3, Ps 123

November 4 2 Kings 17, Hebrews 1, Micah 4, Ps 124

Favorite Verse this Week

November 5 2 Kings 18, Hebrews 2, Micah 5, Ps 125

November 6 2 Kings 19, Hebrews 3, Micah 6, Ps 126

November 7 2 Kings 20, Hebrews 4, Micah 7, Ps 127

November 8 2 Kings 21, Hebrews 5, Nahum 1, Ps 128

November 9 2 Kings 22, Hebrews 6, Nahum 2, Ps 129

November 10 2 Kings 23, Hebrews 7, Nahum 3, Ps 130

November 11 2 Kings 24, Hebrews 8, Hab 1, Ps 131

Favorite Verse this Week

November 12 2 Kings 25, Hebrews 9, Hab 2, Ps 132

November 13 1 Chron 1-2, Heb 10:1 -18, Hab 3,Ps 133

November 14 1 Chron 3-4, Heb 10:19-39, Zeph 1, Ps 134

November 15 1 Chron 5-6, Heb 11:1-19, Zeph 2, Ps 135

November 16 1 Chron 7-8, Heb 11:20-40, Zeph 3, Ps 136

November 17 1 Chron 9-10, Heb 12, Hag 1, Ps 137

November 18 1 Chron 11-12, Hebrews 13, Hag 2, Ps 138

Favorite Verse this Week

November 19 1 Chron13-14, James 1, Zech 1, Ps 139

November 20 1 Chron 15, James 2, Zech 2, Ps 140

November 21 1 Chron 16, James 3, Zech 3, Ps 141

November 22 1 Chron 17, James 4, Zech 4, Ps 142

November 23 1 Chron 18, James 5, Zech 5, Ps 143

November 24 1 Chron 19-20,1 Peter 1, Zech 6,Ps 144

November 25 1 Chron 21, 1 Peter 2, Zech 7, Ps 145

Favorite Verse this Week

November 26 1 Chron 22, 1 Peter 3, Zech 8, Ps 146

November 27 1 Chron 23, 1 Peter 4, Zech 9, Ps 147

November 28 1 Chron 24-25,1 Peter 5, Zech 10, Ps 148

November 29 1 Chron 26-27,2 Peter 1, Zech 11, Ps 149

November 30 1 Chron 28, 2 Peter 2, Zech 12:1-13:1, Ps 150

December 1 1 Chron 29, 2 Peter 3, Zech 13:2-9, Prov 1

December 2 2 Chron 1, John 1, Zech 14, Prov 2

Favorite Verse this Week

December 3 2 Chron 2, 1 John 2, Malachi 1, Prov 3

December 4 2 Chron 3-4, 1 John 3, Malachi 2, Prov 4

December 5 2 Ch 5:1-6:11, 1 John 4, Malachi 3, Prov 5

December 6 2 Ch 6:12-42, 1 John 5, Malachi 4, Prov 6

December 7 2 Chron 7, 2 John, Prov 7

December 8 2 Chron 8, 3 John, Prov 8

December 9 2 Chron 9, Jude, Prov 9

Favorite Verse this Week

December 10 2 Chron 10, Revelation 1, Prov10

December 11 2 Chr11-12, Revelation 2, Prov 11

December 12 2 Chr 13, Revelation 3, Prov 12

December 13 2 Chr14-15, Revelation 4, Prov 13

December 14 2 Chron 16, Revelation 5, Prov 14

December 15 2 Chron 17, Revelation 6, Prov 15

December 16 2 Chron 18, Revelation 7, Prov 16

Favorite Verse this Week

December 17 2Chron 19-20, Revelation 8, Prov 17

December 18 2Chron 21, Revelation 9, Prov 18

December 19 2Chron 22-23, Revelation 10, Prov 19

December 20 2Chr24, Revelation 11, Prov 20

December 21 2Chron 25, Revelation 12, Prov 21

December 22 2Chron 26, Revelation 13, Prov 22

December 23 2Chron 27-28, Revelation 14, Prov 23

Favorite Verse this Week

December 24 2 Chron 29, Revelation 15, Prov 24

December 25 2 Chron 30, Revelation 16, Prov 25

December 26 2 Chron 31, Revelation 17, Prov 26

December 27 2 Chron 32, Revelation 18, Prov 27

December 28 2 Chron 33, Revelation 19, Prov 28

December 29 2 Chron 34, Revelation 20, Prov 29

December 30 2 Chron 35,Revelation 21, Prov 30

December 31 2 Chron 36, Revelation 22, Prov 31

Favorite Verse this Week